IS THERE LIFE WITHOUT DOGS?

by TONI GOFFE

DOGS ARE FOREVER

MW00682577

First published in Great Britain by
Pendulum Gallery Press
56 Ackender Road, Alton, Hants GU34 1JS

© TONI GOFFE 1993

IS THERE LIFE WITHOUT DOGS?
ISBN 0-948912-22-7

All rights reserved. No part of this publication may be reproduced or transmitted in any
form or by any means, electronic or mechanical, including photocopying, recording,
or any information storage and retrieval system, or for a source of ideas without
permission in writing from the publisher

PRINTED IN GREAT BRITAIN BY
UNWIN BROTHERS LTD, OLD WOKING, SURREY

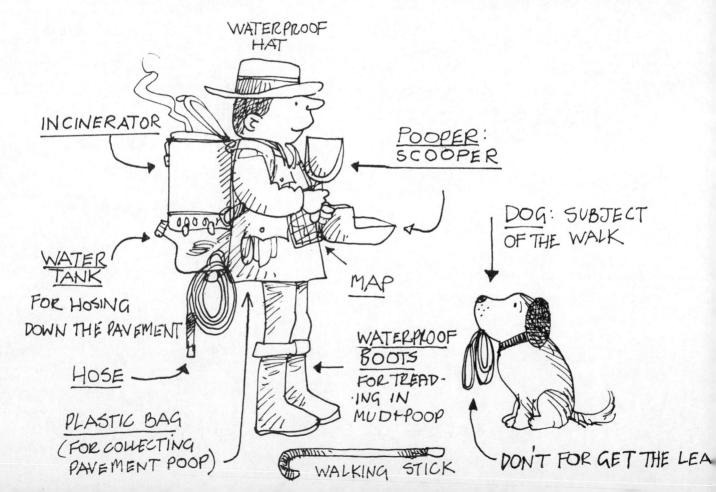

WALKIES: PREPARING TO TAKE YOUR DOG FOR A WALK...

WATERPROOF HAT

INCINERATOR

POOPER: SCOOPER

DOG: SUBJECT OF THE WALK

WATER TANK
FOR HOSING DOWN THE PAVEMENT

MAP

HOSE

WATERPROOF BOOTS FOR TREAD-ING IN MUD+POOP

PLASTIC BAG (FOR COLLECTING PAVEMENT POOP)

WALKING STICK

DON'T FORGET THE LEA

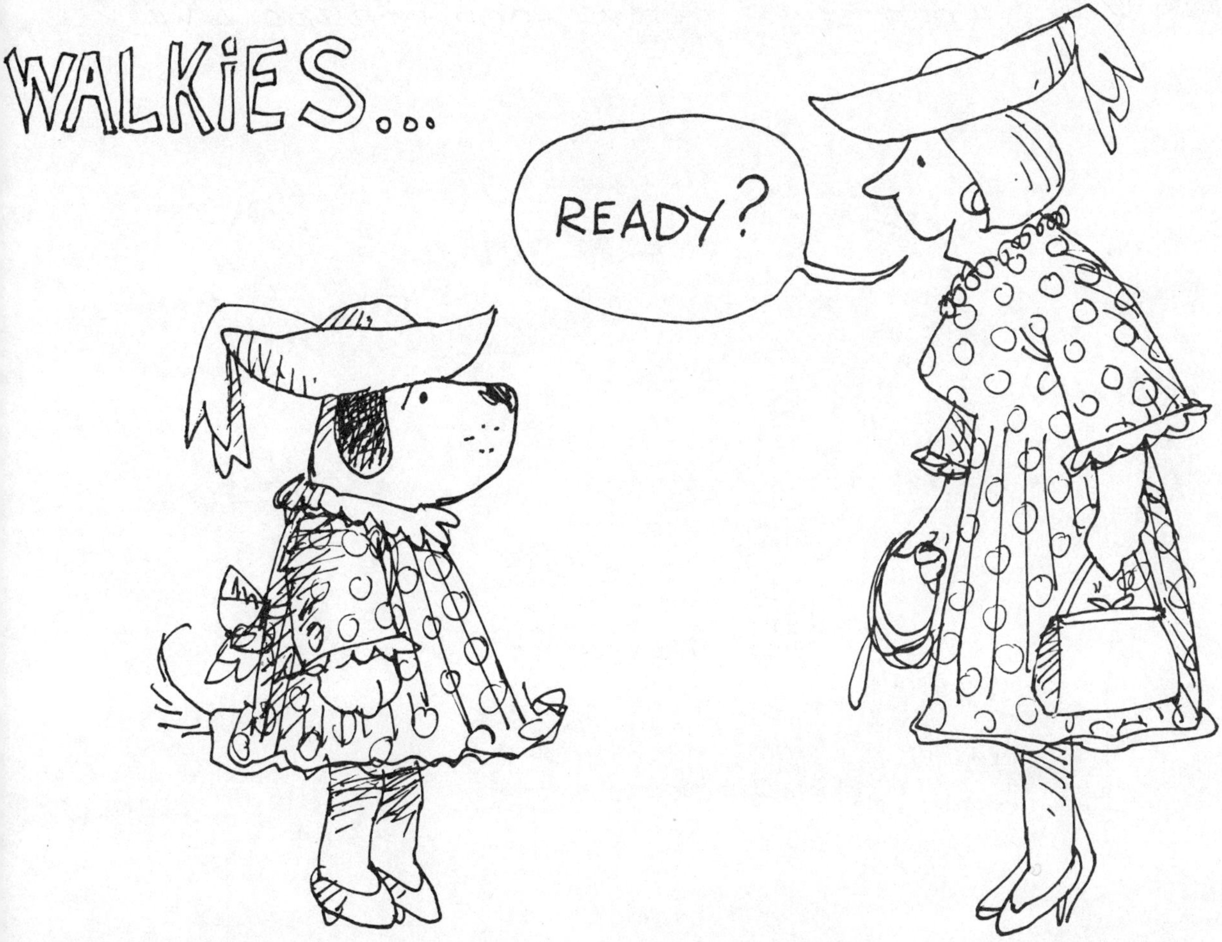
WALKIES...
READY?

TOILET TRAINING YOUR DOG ...

HOW TO STOP YOUR DOG FARTING:

METHOD ONE: (NOT RECOMMENDED)

HOW TO STOP YOUR DOG FARTING:
METHOD TWO: (ALSO NOT RECOMMENDED)

FEED
THIS
END

PREPARE
FOR HEAVY
'BELCHING'
THIS END

HOW TO STOP YOUR DOGS' FARTS FROM SMELLING...

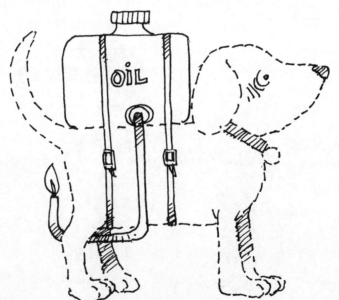

AN EXTRA
LONG LEAD
WOULD BE A
GOOD IDEA....

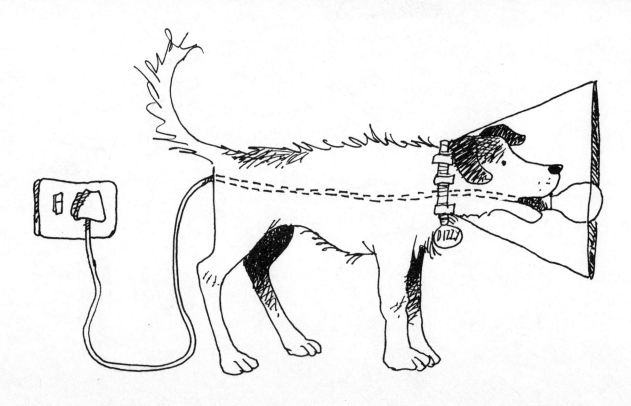

FUN THINGS YOU CAN DO WITH YOUR DOG WHEN
THEY HAVE TO WEAR A PROTECTIVE COLLAR......

DOG PROTECTIVE COLLAR USAGE ....

RALPH, HAVING AN OUT-OF-DOG EXPERIENCE...

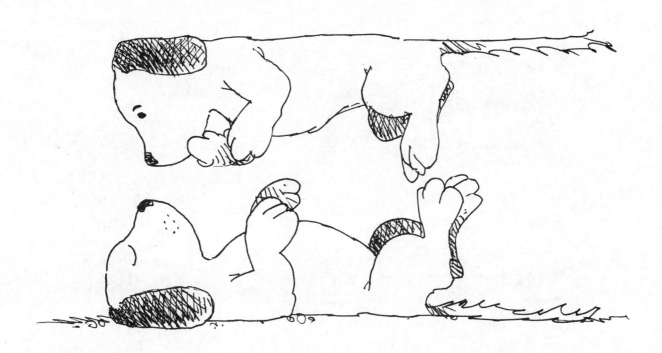

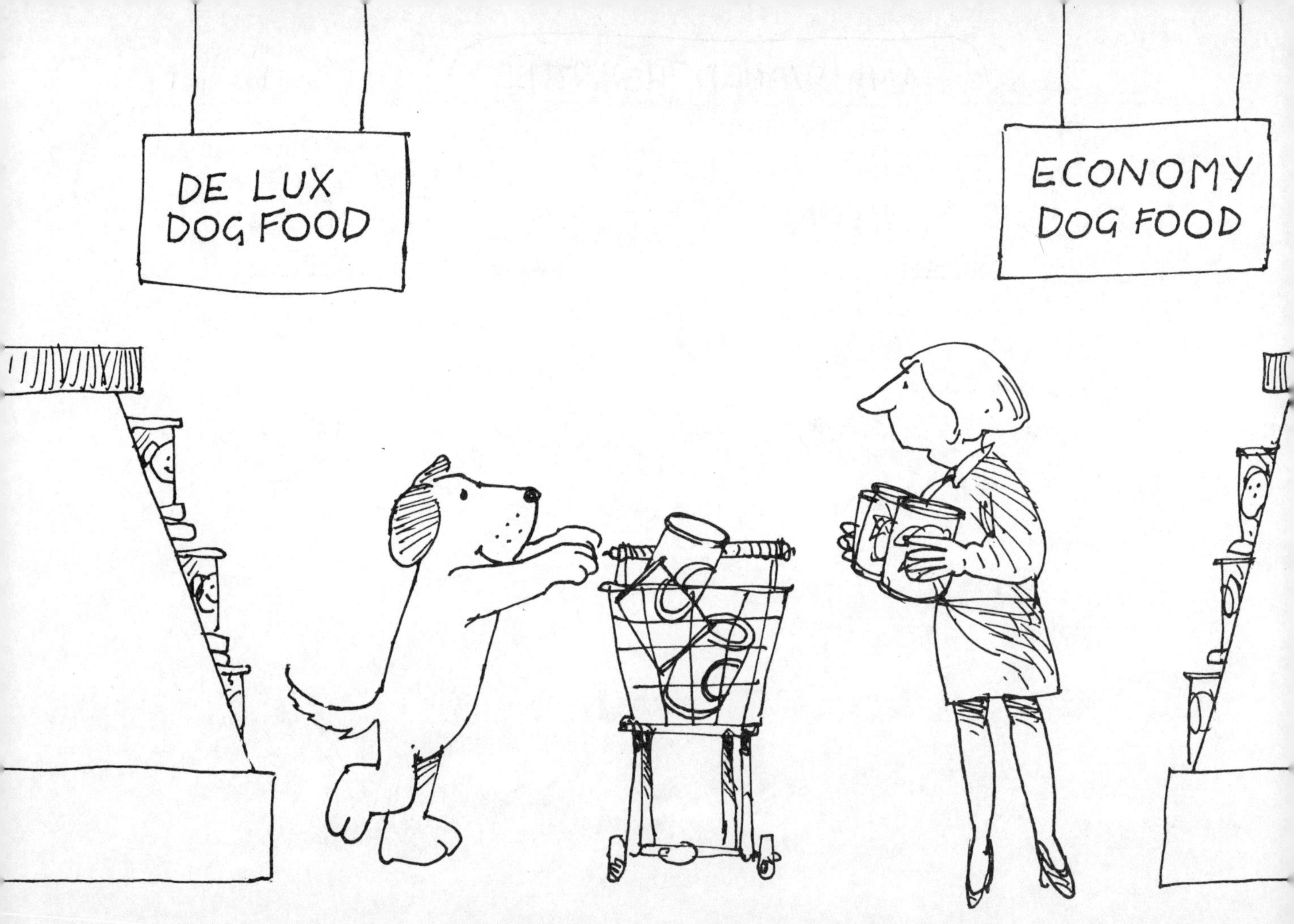
DE LUX
DOG FOOD
ECONOMY
DOG FOOD